P9-DEW-066

空手道
Karate Made Simple

3 Practice, Sparring, and Competition

Maiko Nakashima
with the Japan Karate Federation

The Oliver Press, Inc.
Minneapolis

INTRODUCTION

*K*arate-do is a Japanese *budo*, or martial art. It originated on the Japanese island of Okinawa and spread to the rest of Japan. *Budo* is a part of Japanese culture that is based on traditional combat skills. Like all forms of martial arts, the goal of karate is not just to defeat your opponent; it is also to discipline heart, mind, and body through practice and respect for one's opponents.

Karate-do, or the "way of karate," is now known around the world as "karate." In 2010, the World Karate Federation (WKF) had members in 187 countries, and estimates that around 50 million people study karate. Every two years, there is an international tournament, the World Karate Championships, in which players gather from all over the world to compete.

By reading this book, you will be able to answer these questions:

- **How do you judge the techniques in sparring competition?**
- **What is a "national team"?**
- **Why are warm-up exercises so important?**

Recently, there has been a movement in Japan to place more importance on traditional Japanese culture, including karate. Starting in 2012, all middle-school students were required to take a *budo* class. Imagine being required to take karate as a gym class!

This series is divided into four books that will introduce you to what you need to know to master karate in an easy-to-understand way.

In this series, you will learn how this martial art spread from a small island to become a worldwide phenomenon.

CONTENTS

Training

Karate training is called keiko *in Japan. Here we will describe a typical training routine.*

Training sessions

Workouts typically consist of three parts, which may vary on a given day: warm-up/cool-down exercises, stationary basics, and moving basics. Workouts differ based on the school, the number of practitioners or their level, and sometimes their goals.

A typical training session is shown below. At the beginning and end of practice in a traditional karate school, you sit in *seiza*, where you kneel down and close your eyes to meditate. Training typically lasts an hour; however, sometimes people stay after the workout and continue training.

Warm-up exercises:
Karate is a sport that uses the entire body. It is important to stretch your muscles and joints. If you do warm-up exercises everyday, you will increase your flexibility and reduce your chances of pulling a muscle. You will be able to see the difference when you punch or kick.

Stationary basics:
In this part of training, you work on basic stances, hand and foot position, and techniques such as punches, strikes, kicks, and blocks. You need to pay attention to the target areas of the body during this part of training.

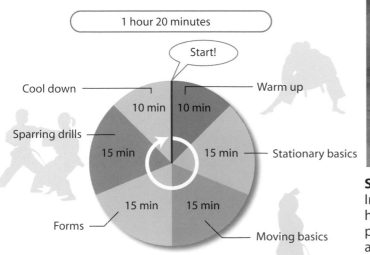

1 hour 20 minutes

Start!

Cool down — 10 min

Warm up

10 min

Sparring drills — 15 min

15 min — Stationary basics

Forms — 15 min

15 min — Moving basics

Moving basics: The same techniques and stances are used as in as stationary practice, but while moving. It is important to maintain balance while you move.

Kata (forms): It is important to understand the meaning of each form (practical application: see book 2) as well as the sequence of movements.

Sparring drills: During this practice you work in pairs to do pre-arranged techniques. These drills help develop a sense of timing and distance.

Kumite (free sparring): In open sparring, attacks and blocks are unscripted. It is very close to an actual sparring competition.

Cool-down exercises: Stretching exercises at the end of the training help increase flexibility and prevent soreness. You may also do muscle training.

"A sport for a lifetime"

In the _dojo_, or training room, you can find every age from children to adults. Some people start karate as seniors and some are children who just started. Karate is a discipline that can be regarded as "a sport for a lifetime."

Some large _dojo_ divide classes according to level or age, but you often see adults and children working together in small _dojo_.

2
Warm-up & Cool-down Exercises

Warm-up and cool-down exercises are an important part of a rigorous workout.

Why are warm-ups necessary?

Body movements come from the muscles contracting and relaxing. However, if you start working out without stretching the muscles first, this can lead to an injury. It is important to warm up and stretch before the actual training session.

It is also necessary to do a cool-down exercise after the training. This helps the muscles to recover. In fact, stretching out after a workout may increase flexibility even more than stretching beforehand!

How to stretch

Stretching is the core exercise in warm-up and cool-down exercises. There are two types of stretching. One stretches the muscles without moving and the other stretches by moving your body. Here we will show you several stationary stretches. Please keep in mind the following points:

- Remember to breathe. Breathe out as you go into a stretch.
- Pay attention to the parts that are stretched.
- Stretch slowly. Hold each stretch for about 15 seconds.
- Do not strain your muscles. Stretch just to the point right before it starts to hurt.
- Do right and left sides equally.

DID YOU KNOW?
Warm-up exercises

Karate is a sport that uses all parts of the body. It is important to loosen your muscles before working out in order to avoid injuries. Stretching every day with an appropriate warm-up will improve your ability to execute proper technique.

● Hamstring and groin

Squat on one leg with the other leg extended. Lean over the extended knee for a better stretch.

● Hip flexor

Stand as if taking a big step. Bend front leg.

Do not stick your buttocks out.

● Groin muscles, hip joints

Put soles of your feet together. Knees are close to the floor. Lean forward while pressing legs down.

● Ankle

Sit down and rotate the ankle using your hands. Rotate forwards and backwards.

● Quadriceps

Bend one knee. Sit down with your other leg straight. Lean backwards.

Stop the body before the knees lift up.

● Stomach

Start from face-down position. Arch back by supporting your upper body with both hands.

Stop before your stomach lifts off from the floor.

● Shoulder

Pull your body back with both your hands and knees on the floor.

Bring your shoulder closer to the floor.

Keep elbows straight.

● Back and hips

Lie down facing up. Bring both feet over your head.

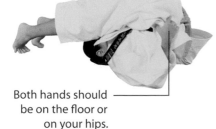

Both hands should be on the floor or on your hips.

● Back of shoulder

Extend one arm and pull it close to your chest with the other arm.

Back of the hand of your stretched arm should face front.

Do not lift your shoulder.

● Triceps stretch

Bend your arm and bring it behind your head. Pull elbow using your other hand.

Bend elbow as far down as you can.

Stretch your armpit muscles by moving your body in the direction of the arrow.

Do not lift your shoulder.

Stationary Basics

Here we will learn the basic stances and techniques while staying in one position.

The goal of stationary basics

Stationary practice allows you to master the details of each technique. Repeated practice develops "muscle memory" so that you can react instinctively, accurately, and powerfully in a more high-pressure situation.

● How to deliver a punch*:

1 Make fist correctly in the right stance.

2 Extend your fist with the palm down.

3 At the same time, pull your other fist close to the ribs with the palm facing up.

4 Punch forward with the rear fist while rotating it from palm up to palm down. At the same time, pull your other fist close to the ribs.

The foundational skills you develop during stationary practice will be built upon during moving basics. The stances you learn will also be applied in sparring, when you are required to move around. Stationary practice will help you acquire the fundamentals of hand and foot position, stance, posture, and how to bow.

*see books 1 and 2 for details.

About stationary basics

Repetition is very important. It allows you to focus on one technique at a time. You can also learn to deliver the same technique in different ways. For instance, a punch could be thrown as a front or reverse punch, and it could be directed high or to the midsection.

Main techniques of stationary basics

·······▶ Next move ──────▶ Previous move ⌑ Striking surface

● Middle punch

— Natural stance

● Middle punch

— Square stance

This is a punch to the middle of the body. It can be used against other parts of the body as well.

● Rising block

Rising block defends the upper part of the body.

● Middle inside block

● Middle outside block

● Downward (low) block

● Knifehand block

See book 2 for a full description of stances and techniques.

● Front kick

● Side kick

A side kick is usually aimed at the middle of the body, but sometimes is aimed at the head or knee.

9

Moving Basics

Moving basics expand on the fundamental techniques learned in the stationary position. They add movement back and forth.

The goal of moving basics

In a real fight, you would never stand still. Therefore, it is important to learn to do techniques while moving. Moving basics help you to learn the most efficient ways to move your body while executing the techniques. Quick, smooth movements will enable you to generate a powerful punch or kick. All techniques require you to keep your body balanced and stable.

About moving basics

Beginners often practice moving back and forth with their hands on their hips. As you get used to this movement, you can add techniques such as throwing a punch while taking a step forward. You will execute the same techniques as you learned during stationary basics. If you practice in a small *dojo*, you will need to learn to turn frequently when you reach the end of the room. Here we show you how to combine moving forward while punching with turning 180° and stepping back.

Forward movement with front punch

········► Next move
———► Previous move
······► Keep moving.

1

Keep your body straight and centered.

Keep your hips steady. Do not move up and down.

Shift into a deep front stance.

2

Do not move your hand up or down.

Put weight on your front foot. Move the back foot forward in a semicircular motion under you. This will help you stay balanced.

Keep ball of the foot on the floor while you slide it forward.

Changing position

1 Punch with your right hand.

2 Raise left fist up to your right shoulder.

3 As you turn 180° counterclockwise, do a downwards circular block with your left hand.

Left foot in front.

You can also change position by moving your front foot sideways. There are different ways to move your arms, too.

DID YOU KNOW?
What does "ossu" mean?

You may hear a lot of calling "osu" (oh-soo) or "ossu" (ohs-soo) at the beginning of practice. "Ossu" is used as a greeting which is similar to "hi." Since the kanji character of "tolerant" reads as "osu" in Japanese, some people say that it originated from that word. However, there are other theories about where it came from, too.

Backward movement with rising block

1 RISING BLOCK

Move center of the body without stopping the movement.

Front stance

Shift weight to your left foot, and bring your right foot back in a curved path underneath your body.

2 RISING BLOCK

Pull right fist back to the hip while blocking with the left hand.

Body remains upright while shifting back and blocking in one continuous movement.

3 Move forward in one continuous motion.

4 Prepare to punch while shifting your weight forward.

The ball of your foot brushes the floor as you step forward.

5 FRONT PUNCH

Do not lean forward.

Punch while stepping forward.

Sparring Drills

Yakusoku kumite, or sparring drills, are exercises that are performed one-on-one. Because the moves are predetermined, they are called sparring drills.

The goal of sparring drills

The purpose of sparring drills is to learn how to execute techniques such as punches, kicks, or blocks accurately with a real opponent. The goal is to execute each technique as if you were in a real fight. By testing your techniques against an opponent, you can develop timing and a sense of distance that would be useful in case you were ever in a real fight.

Types of sparring drills

Sparring drills are done in pairs. One person attacks, and then the other person defends, in a predetermined sequence of movements. It is important to be able to perform techniques with both sides of the body, so if you throw a right front punch, then you need to practice with the left front punch as well. After practicing with both hands, attacker and defender switch roles and practice the same drill. Here we will show you four main patterns of sparring drills. All drills start with *rei*.

Children training with a *ki-yaah*!

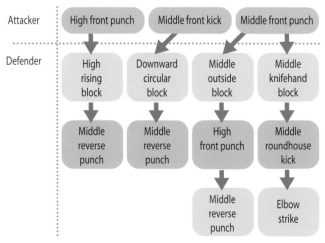

Attacker	High front punch	Middle front kick	Middle front punch	
Defender	High rising block	Downward circular block	Middle outside block	Middle knifehand block
	Middle reverse punch	Middle reverse punch	High front punch	Middle roundhouse kick
			Middle reverse punch	Elbow strike

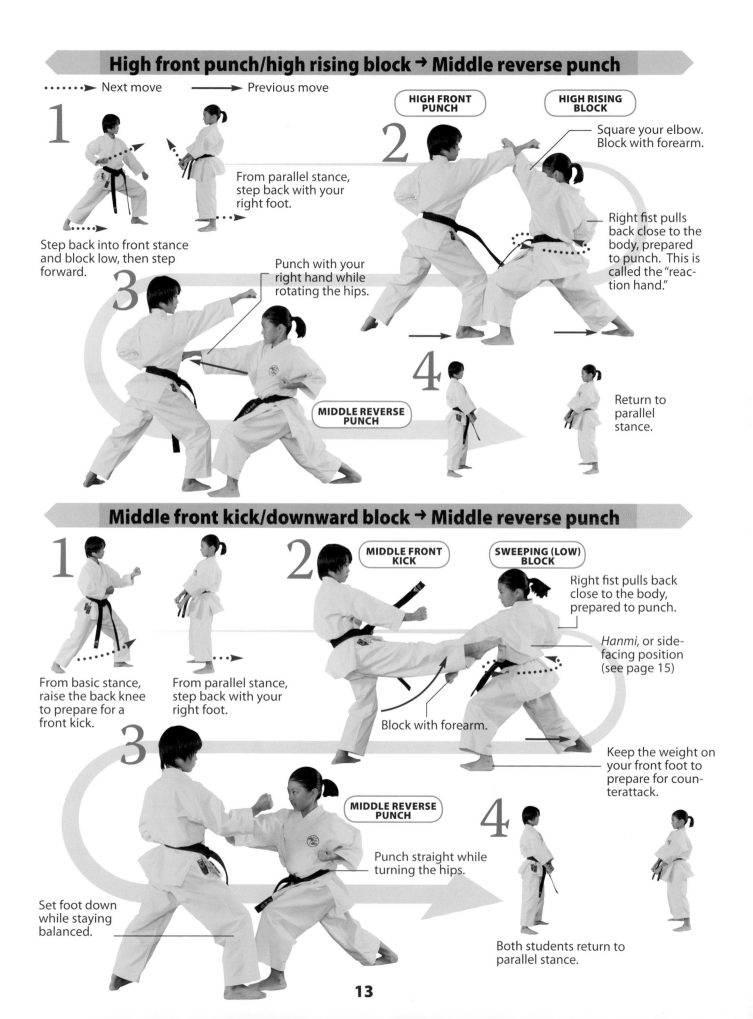

High front punch/high rising block → Middle reverse punch

······► Next move ────► Previous move

1 Step back into front stance and block low, then step forward.

From parallel stance, step back with your right foot.

2 **HIGH FRONT PUNCH** **HIGH RISING BLOCK**

Square your elbow. Block with forearm.

Right fist pulls back close to the body, prepared to punch. This is called the "reaction hand."

3 Punch with your right hand while rotating the hips.

MIDDLE REVERSE PUNCH

4 Return to parallel stance.

Middle front kick/downward block → Middle reverse punch

1 From basic stance, raise the back knee to prepare for a front kick.

From parallel stance, step back with your right foot.

2 **MIDDLE FRONT KICK** **SWEEPING (LOW) BLOCK**

Right fist pulls back close to the body, prepared to punch.

Hanmi, or side-facing position (see page 15)

Block with forearm.

Keep the weight on your front foot to prepare for counterattack.

3 Set foot down while staying balanced.

MIDDLE REVERSE PUNCH

Punch straight while turning the hips.

4 Both students return to parallel stance.

13

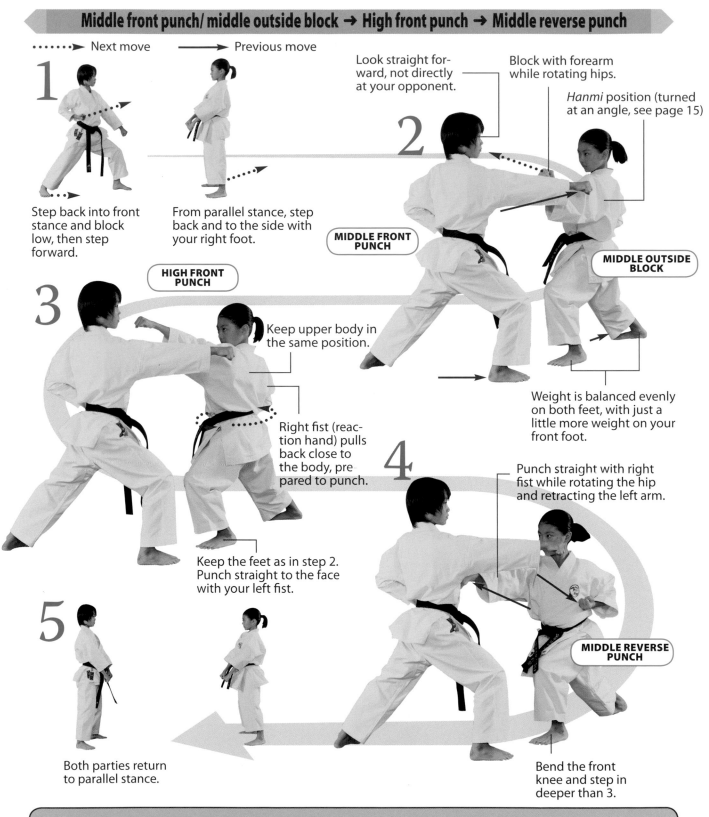

········▶ Next move   ──────▶ Previous move

1

Step back into front stance and block low, then step forward.

From parallel stance, step back and to the side with your right foot.

2

Look straight forward, not directly at your opponent.

Block with forearm while rotating hips.

Hanmi position (turned at an angle, see page 15)

MIDDLE FRONT PUNCH

MIDDLE OUTSIDE BLOCK

Weight is balanced evenly on both feet, with just a little more weight on your front foot.

3

HIGH FRONT PUNCH

Keep upper body in the same position.

Right fist (reaction hand) pulls back close to the body, prepared to punch.

Keep the feet as in step 2. Punch straight to the face with your left fist.

4

Punch straight with right fist while rotating the hip and retracting the left arm.

MIDDLE REVERSE PUNCH

5

Both parties return to parallel stance.

Bend the front knee and step in deeper than 3.

Zanshin -"Relaxed awareness" or poise and control

In karate, it is important to stay alert and on guard even after an attack. This is called *zanshin*, a state of physical and mental preparedness. *Zanshin* is an important mental state which can affect the outcome of sparring competitions. Judges take into account whether they observe *zanshin* while the athletes demonstrate techniques.

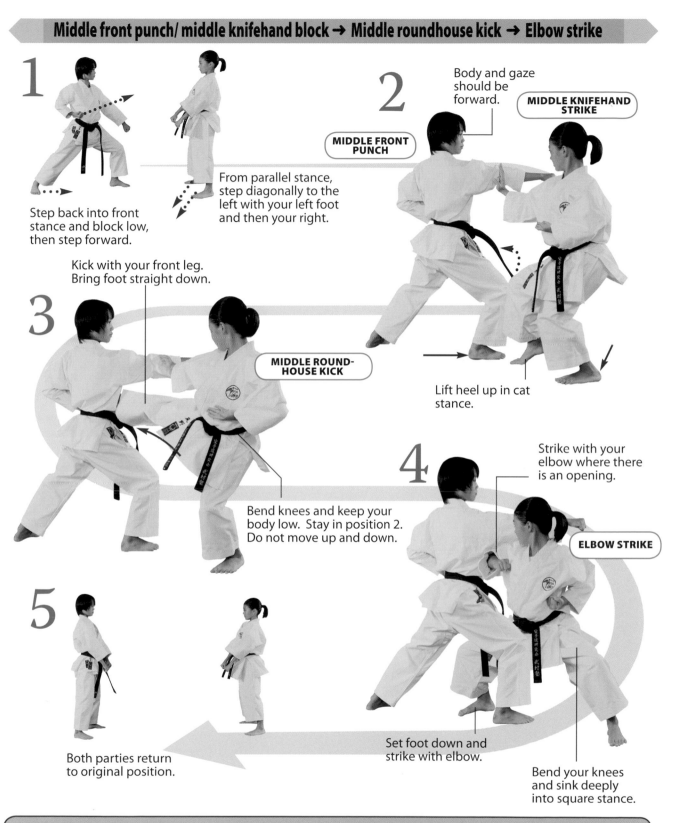

1

Step back into front stance and block low, then step forward.

2

Body and gaze should be forward.

MIDDLE KNIFEHAND STRIKE

MIDDLE FRONT PUNCH

From parallel stance, step diagonally to the left with your left foot and then your right.

Lift heel up in cat stance.

3

Kick with your front leg. Bring foot straight down.

MIDDLE ROUND-HOUSE KICK

Bend knees and keep your body low. Stay in position 2. Do not move up and down.

4

Strike with your elbow where there is an opening.

ELBOW STRIKE

Set foot down and strike with elbow.

Bend your knees and sink deeply into square stance.

5

Both parties return to original position.

Hanmi - Side-facing position

Turning your body diagonally towards your opponent is called *hanmi* (hahn-me). It gives your opponent fewer targets and makes it more difficult to see your attacks coming. As you circle with an opponent in sparring, your ability to maintain this position by turning your hips smoothly is vital to competing well. Facing your opponent directly, on the other hand, is called *mami* (mah-me) or "square facing."

Free Sparring

In sparring drills, movements are predetermined. In kumite, *or free sparring, attack and counterattack are spontaneous.*

Key points of sparring practice

In sparring practice, attacks and blocks are freely exchanged with your opponent. It is important for you to close the distance with your opponent to attack quickly, then retreat before a counterattack can be thrown. This requires a good sense of distance and timing.

Positioning and footwork

Positioning and footwork are very important to maintaining proper distancing and timing.

Your positioning should allow you to be ready for both offense and defense. You can move freely forward and back, sideways or diagonally, as if you are tapping a rhythm with your feet. This is called footwork. When executed with the right timing, it allows you to get close enough to the opponent to perform effective techniques.

Freestyle posture in sparring

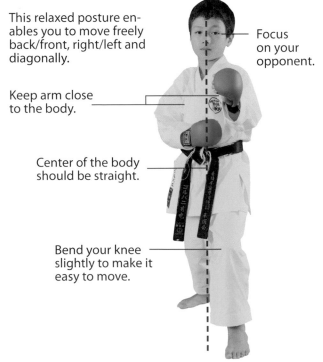

This relaxed posture enables you to move freely back/front, right/left and diagonally.

Keep arm close to the body.

Center of the body should be straight.

Bend your knee slightly to make it easy to move.

Focus on your opponent.

Back/front footwork

In order to adjust the distance between you and your opponent, you should create a rhythm with your feet by moving back and forth. You need to keep your upper body stable. Head and eye direction should not change.

Next move ••••••••►
Previous move ————►

1

Create rhythm with footwork.

Move back

2

Move forward.

3

Keep the center of your body stable while moving.

Sideways footwork

In order to create an opening to attack, shift sideways back and forth using footwork. You need to keep your upper body stable. Head and eye direction should not change.

1

Create rhythm with footwork.

2

Step in wide to the side.

3

Shift weight to leading foot. Pull trailing foot in to return to initial position.

4

Return to position 1.

 # Sparring

After mastering stance and footwork, now we enter into the actual practice of *kumite*, or sparring. The sequence on the right shows the basics of delivering a technique. Here we will show you the jab and reverse punch so you can master the basics.

1 Use footwork to create an opening to attack.

2 Take a deep step in to get closer to your opponent, and attack.

3 Pull back your fist or kick immediately after the attack.

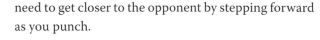 ## Jab

A jab is thrown by punching in a straight line with the leading hand. Starting from the basic position, you need to get closer to the opponent by stepping forward as you punch.

······▶ Next move   ⟶ Previous move ·····▶ Do not stop moving.

1 Move freely.

Find the right timing with footwork.

2 Punch straight forward from the initial position. Do not pull back your elbow before the punch.

Lunge forward with your front foot to get closer to the opponent.

Pull back your fist immediately.

JAB

Shift weight briefly to front foot as you jab.

The above picture shows a high jab.

3 Return to the initial position and prepare for the next attack.

18

Reverse punch

To deliver a reverse punch, you step forward and punch with the hand opposite the lead foot.

This technique is widely used to score points in sparring competition.

1 Move freely.

Use footwork to find the right moment to attack.

2

Step in deeply with your front foot to get closer to the opponent.

Pull your fist back immediately.

REVERSE PUNCH

Punch straight forward at the same time while rotating your hip. Do not pull back your elbow before punching. This picture shows a reverse punch to the middle of the body. However, you can punch high as well.

Position yourself in *hanmi* and return hips to their initial position. Prepare for the opponent's next attack.

3

Shift back with footwork.

Combination techniques

After mastering the basic techniques, you can combine them. Here we will show you the combination of a jab and a reverse punch.

Jab → Reverse punch

This is a combination of two punches. Immediately after the jab, a reverse punch is delivered by stepping forward.

········► Next move   ──────► Previous move

1 Move freely.

Use footwork to find the right moment to attack.

2 Take a step to get closer to the opponent.

3 Punch straight forward with your lead hand. Do not pull your elbow back before punching.

After the punch, bring your rear foot half a foot closer to the front foot. Do it quickly.

JAB

4 Pull back your fist immediately.

Start the reverse punch as you pull back your lead hand.

After bringing your rear foot closer to the front, step in deeply with your front foot.

5 **REVERSE PUNCH**

Punch with your right hand while turning your hips.

Step down as you throw the punch.

6 Pull your fist back quickly and prepare for the next attack.

Shift back using footwork after throwing the reverse punch.

The above picture shows a high jab and a reverse punch to the midsection. You can use these techniques to attack other parts of the body as well.

Reverse punch → Roundhouse kick

This is a combination of a punch and a kick. Divert the opponent with a punch and attack with a kick.

1 Move freely.

Use footwork to create the right distance and timing for an attack.

2 REVERSE PUNCH

Punch with your rear hand while moving in towards your opponent. Pull fist back immediately.

After the punch, bring your rear foot quickly to the front.

3 Look at your opponent.

Shift weight to your front foot as your rear foot passes it.

4 ROUND KICK

Execute roundhouse kick while turning your hip over. Pull your foot back immediately.

The above picture shows a reverse punch to the midsection and a high roundhouse kick. You can attack other parts of the body as well.

5

6 Shift feet back.

 # Counterattacks

After mastering combinations, you will learn how to counterattack. This is the practice of deflecting or blocking your opponent's attack and delivering your attack at the same time. There are a variety of ways to respond depending on the type of attack.

Jab /deflection → Reverse punch

Deflect the opponent's punch and counterattack with a reverse punch to the opponent's unguarded midsection.

······▶ Next move   ⟶ Previous move ·····▶ Keep moving

1 Move freely

Use footwork to find an opening.

2

3

JAB
(see page 18)

DEFLECTION

Avoid the punch coming right at you by deflecting the attack.

REVERSE PUNCH

Punch straight forward while deflecting the jab. Pull back immediately after delivering the punch.

Step in to get within striking distance.

4

Move back with footwork.

DID YOU KNOW?
What is a "pre-emptive strike" versus a "counterattack"?

A pre-emptive strike means to attack at the first sign of aggression from your opponent. A counterattack means to allow your opponent to attack first so as to open up targets for response. Both tactics are important in *kumite*. You need to judge timing and distance to deliver techniques when your opponent is off-guard.

Application

In a real *kumite* competition, athletes use a variety of techniques. Here we will show you a sequence of attacks and counterattacks.

Jab/deflection → Roundhouse kick

It is important to execute the roundhouse kick immediately after deflecting your opponent's attack.

1 Move freely.

Use footwork to create an opening.

2 JAB   DEFLECTION

3 REVERSE PUNCH

DEFLECTION
Deflect the opponent's punch.

Take a step to your left as you block.

4 Focus on your opponent.

Prepare to kick with your right leg by shifting weight to your left leg.

5 Deliver roundhouse kick as you turn your hip.

ROUNDHOUSE KICK

6 Pull your leg back immediately and prepare for the opponent's counterattack.

Shift feet back.

Kumite Competition

Karate competitions consist of **kumite** *(sparring) and* **kata** *(forms). In* **kumite,** *points are awarded when you succeed in attacking the opponent.*

What exactly is *kumite* competition?

Kumite competition is when athletes spar against a partner to gain points. The first athlete to be ahead by eight points wins. Otherwise, whoever has the most points when the time has expired wins. To be awarded points, you need to deliver a controlled technique successfully to one of the seven parts of the body shown below.

Controlled technique means the skill to stop the attack at the moment of contact. In sparring competitions, contact is prohibited. Only those who are able to control their actions fully are regarded as masters of the art.

For a technique to be awarded a point, it must meet the standards shown below. When a technique is delivered successfully, the judge will decide whether it counts as a full point, half point, or valid; the one who executed the technique will get the point.

● Target areas

Head
Face
Neck
Chest
Ribs
Back
Abdomen

● Point decision standards:

Correct form/ Good sportsmanship / Vigorous application / Physical and mental awareness / Appropriate timing / Proper distance

● Point system:

3 points (full point – *ippon*)	• high kick. • any technique delivered on a thrown or fallen opponent.
2 points (half point – *waza ari*)	• midsection kick
1 point (valid – *yuko*)	• punch or strike to one of the 7 areas of the body.

Kumite competitions

Kumite competition consists of both team and individual matches. The individual matches are typically separated into age and weight divisions. Competitors wear either a red belt and pads, or blue belt and pads. Belts showing rank are not worn.

Each match begins with a *rei* or bow (see book 1). Sparring begins as soon as the referee calls, "Start the match." A round is 3 minutes for men and 2 minutes for women and those under 21 years of age.

In team competitions, male teams field five athletes in each round. Female teams field three athletes in a given round.

Judge

Sparring matches are judged by one head referee, three assistant referees, and an arbitrator. In *kata* competition, five people (one head judge and four assistant judges) use red and blue flags to determine the points (see pages 26 and 27).

In international competitions, judges cannot be from the same country as an athlete they are judging.

The judges must wear the designated uniform provided by the sponsoring organization.

Prohibited acts and penalties

There are two categories of penalties in sparring competition. The penalty given for Category 1 violations depends on the severity of the violation. In Category 2, a warning is given if the violation level is low and it is the first time. If the violation occurs for a second time or the violation level is high, a second warning is given and the opponent receives 1 point. For the third violation, a penalty warning is given and the opponent receives 2 points. A fourth violation will cause the athlete to forfeit the match.

● Prohibited acts

■ Category 1 (Actions that could injure opponent):

① Hitting opponent with excessive force or attacking the throat.

② Attacking the arms, legs, groin, joints, or instep.

③ Open-hand attack to the face.

④ Dangerous or prohibited throwing techniques.

■ Category 2 (Other actions):

① Pretending to be hurt or exaggerating injury.

② Going out of bounds repeatedly.

③ Deliberately exposing yourself to injury.

④ Avoiding combat to keep your opponent from scoring.

⑤ Pushing, grabbing, or tackling the opponent without delivering a technique.

⑥ Executing dangerous techniques or uncontrolled attacks.

⑦ Attacking with your head, knee, or elbow.

⑧ Disrespectful or rude behavior to a referee or your opponent.

Kata Competition

Kata competitors demonstrate accuracy, power and speed as they perform a set pattern of techniques. Judges hold up colored flags to vote for the competitor they feel performed the best.

Kata and competition

Every karate student learns *kata*, or forms. *Kata* are a set sequence of movements that include attack and defense against one or several imaginary attackers. Since basic techniques such as punches, strikes, kicks, and blocks are covered in the patterns, practicing these forms is a means of staying true to karate's origins.

In competitions, atheletes are judged on accuracy, speed, and power as they perform the patterns.

This statement by the World Karate Federation defines the essence of *kata*:

Kata *is not a dance or theatrical performance. It must adhere to the traditional values and principles. It must be realistic in fighting terms and display concentration, power, and potential impact in its techniques. It must demonstrate strength, power, and speed — as well as grace, rhythm, and balance.*

The picture below shows a team performing *kata*. In *kata* competition, the three-person team is either all male or all female.

Kata competition

In *kata* competition, athletes are separated into red and blue groups and demonstrate in a certain order. The way to start the match is shown below.

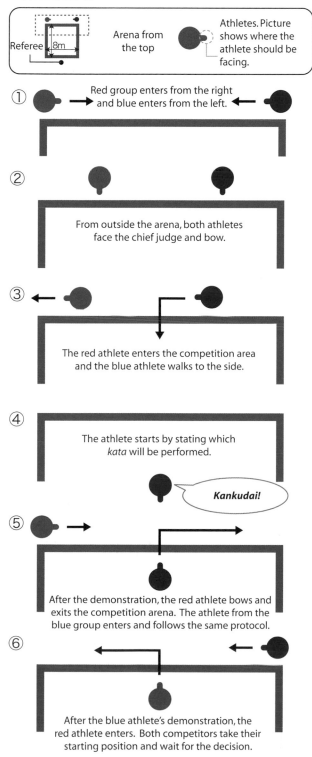

① Red group enters from the right and blue enters from the left.

② From outside the arena, both athletes face the chief judge and bow.

③ The red athlete enters the competition area and the blue athlete walks to the side.

④ The athlete starts by stating which *kata* will be performed.

Kankudai!

⑤ After the demonstration, the red athlete bows and exits the competition arena. The athlete from the blue group enters and follows the same protocol.

⑥ After the blue athlete's demonstration, the red athlete enters. Both competitors take their starting position and wait for the decision.

*When two athletes perform at the same time, both walk up to the center. The red athlete states the *kata* they will be demonstrating.

Standards for decision

The winner is determined by five judges. Each judge raises either a red or blue flag. The athlete who gets the most votes is declared the winner.

● Standards for decision

① A realistic demonstration of the form's meaning.
② Understanding of the techniques being used.
③ Good timing, rhythm, speed, balance, and focus of power.
④ Proper use of breathing as an aid to focus power.
⑤ Correct focus of attention and concentration.
⑥ Correct stances with proper tension in the legs.
⑦ Proper tension in the abdomen and no bobbing up and down of the hips when moving.
⑧ Correct form of the style being demonstrated.
⑨ In team competition, synchronization without external cues.

What is a national team?

A national team is a group of athletes selected from a given country to participate in international competitions around the world. How is the national team selected? What kind of activities does it participate in?

National team and representative athletes

A national team usually consists of a country's best athletes. They represent their country in international competitions.

National teams are formed for many sports such as soccer and swimming, and compete at the international level. Their members are called representative athletes. In the U.S., representative athletes are selected by the USA National Karate-do Federation (USA-NKF).

Athletes are selected from U.S. Team Trial competitions held at the same time as the U.S. National Karate Championships. This is organized by the USA-NKF once a year in July. The top eight athletes in each state/regional competition advance to the National Championships. Two Open Competitions offer additional opportunities to earn a spot at the national team trials.

What are the different age divisions?

Each karate organization has its own age divisions. Some start as young as five years old. Typically, though, competitors are divided into the age categories shown below.

Youth	under 18 years old
Adult	18-34 years old
Senior	35+ years old

Competitors may also be classified into weight or rank divisions. A Senior can compete in the Adult category, but younger competitors cannot move up to the Senior division.

Who is eligible for the National Team?
- The top competitors in each division from the previous year's National Championship.
- The top competitors in each division in the current year's National Karate Championships.
- The makeup of the team may change from one competition to the next if a member is injured or unable to compete for some reason.

What do representative athletes do?

In Japan, representative athletes participate in an intense training camp run by the Japan Karate Federation once a month. They sometimes travel overseas to participate in joint training sessions with national teams from other countries.

Athletes can become more motivated and improve their skills by training with other world-class athletes and experiencing different practice environments.

What is expected by the National Team?

Karate emphasizes the spirit of honoring those people who have contributed to your success. You should remember to be appreciative and respectful of your instructors, juniors, family, and fans.

Members of the national team are role models for children who aim to be successful athletes. Successful athletes are required to be respectful to others as well and mature in their actions. With these ideals in mind, athletes around the world train hard every day to achieve their dreams.

Nurturing future athletes

One way to promote karate is for National Team athletes and their coaches to visit gym classes around the country. This allows students to see world-class athletes and techniques in person, and can generate tremendous enthusiasm for the sport.

Former representative athlete Azusa Tomishiro instructs younger students.

INDEX

GLOSSARY

Japanese Transliteration	Pronunciation	Meaning
Karatedo	*Karate-doe*	Way of karate
Budo	*Boo-doe*	Martial arts
Keiko	*Kay-koh*	Training, practice
Kata	*Kah-tah*	Practice form
Dojo	*Doe-joe*	Training room
Ossu	*Ohs-soo*	Greeting in karate (Hi)
Yakusoku kumite	*Yah-koo-soh-koo Koo-me-teh*	Sparring drills
Kumite	*Koo-me-teh*	Free sparring
Zanshin	*Zahn-shen*	Poise and control
Hanmi	*Hahn-me*	Side facing position
Mami	*Mah-me*	Square facing position
Ippon	*Ipp-pon*	Full point
Waza ari	*Wah-zah ah-ree*	Half point
Yuko	*Yoo-koh*	Valid point

WEBSITES

Karate World:
http://www.karatedo.co.jp/index3.htm

World Karate Federation:
http://www.wkf.net/index.php

Japan Karatedo Federation:
http://www.karatedo.co.jp/jkf/jkf-eng/e_index.htm

This edition published in 2013 by The Oliver Press, Inc.
Charlotte Square
5707 West 36th Street
Minneapolis, MN 55416-2510

KARATE MADE SIMPLE: PRACTICE, SPARRING, AND COMPETITION

Original Japanese title: KIHON WO KIWAMERU! KARATEDO: KEIKO TO KYOUGI
(Mastering the Basics! Karatedo: Practice and Competition)
© Champ Co., Ltd., 2011
All rights reserved.
Original Japanese edition published in 2011 by Champ Co., Ltd.
English translation rights with Imajinsha Co., Ltd. through Japan UNI Agency, Inc., Tokyo

Library of Congress Cataloging-in-Publication Data

Nakashima, Maiko.
Karate made simple 3 : practice, sparring and competition / Maiko Nakashima with the Japan Karate Federation.
    p. cm. -- (Karate made simple)
Includes bibliographical references and index.
ISBN 978-1-934545-19-5
1. Karate--Juvenile literature. I. Title.
GV1114.3.N3426 2012
796.815'3--dc23
                    2012033030

Text: Maiko Nakashima with the Japan Karate Federation
Translation: Chiaki Hasegawa and Goldie Gibbs
U.S. editing: April Stern
U.S. production: Clay Schotzko

Picture Credits:
All images courtesy of Champ Co., Ltd. and Imajinsha Co., Ltd.

ISBN: 978-1-934545-19-5
Printed in the United States of America
17 16 15 14 13   8 7 6 5 4 3 2 1